Happy Days

Happy Days

A UNICEF Book of Birthdays
Name Days and Growing Days

Written and Illustrated by
Christine Price

Published by

UNITED STATES COMMITTEE FOR UNICEF

UNITED NATIONS, NEW YORK

acknowledgments

P. 9 and p. 11, from *The Gift Is Rich* by E. Russell Carter, New York, Friendship Press, 1955; p. 15, from *The Masai; Herders of East Africa* by Sonia Bleeker. New York, William Morrow, 1963; p. 22, from *Egyptian Folk Songs* compiled by Baheega Sidky Rasheed. Cairo, 1958; p. 28, from *Southeast Asian Birth Customs* by Donn V. Hart and others. New Haven, Human Relations Area Files Press, 1965; p. 42, from *A Japanese Miscellany* by Lafcadio Hearn. Boston, Little, Brown and Co., 1901; p. 44, from *The Chinese Classics* edited by James Legge. Vol. IV. London, Trubner and Co., 1871; pps. 46-47, from "The Omaha Tribe" by Alice C. Fletcher and Francis LaFlesche. 27th Annual Report of the Bureau of American Ethnology, 1905-1906. Washington, D. C., Government Printing Office, 1911; p. 53, from *Children's Songs from Japan* by Florence White and Kazuo Akiyama. New York, Edward B. Marks Music Corp., 1960; p. 65, from *Folksongs and Games of Holland* collected and arranged by Ann E. Roeder, New York, G. Schirmer, 1956; p. 77, Oficina de Distribucion de Publicaciones, Ministerio de Relaciones Exteriores, Caracas; p. 104, from *A Treasury of Mexican Folkways* by Francis Toor. New York, Crown Publishers, 1947.

Contents

Introduction

For families in all parts of the world, there are very special happy days. This book tells about some of these important times—the day when a cherished new baby is given his name—the celebration of a child's birthday anniversary—a ceremony of growing up, when a young person is initiated into adult responsibilities in his society or religion. Whatever form this occasion may take, it is a landmark in the life of the child, a day of great meaning and joy for his family. Even though you will find that many of the customs differ around the world, there is one universal similarity common to all cultures—the great importance of the child to his family.

Children also hold a special place in the lives of the nations in which they are growing up, for it is they ultimately who will shape their countries' future. The task of UNICEF, the United Nations Children's Fund, is to help the less developed nations of the world to overcome the problems their children face. UNICEF helps protect their children from hunger and illness and better prepare them to take their place as useful adults in their societies.

The U.S. Committee for UNICEF is indebted to Christine Price, who, as a labor of love, has written, illustrated and designed this important book for UNICEF as her contribution to children in need.

Our hope in presenting this book—and UNICEF's hope in its work throughout the world—is that the life journeys of all children will be filled with happy days.

MRS. GUIDO PANTALEONI, JR.
President,
United States Committee for UNICEF

Grandfather, Great Spirit, all over the world the faces of living ones are alike. With tenderness have they come up out of the ground. Look upon your children, with children in their arms, that they may face the winds and walk the good road to the day of quiet.

Grandfather, Great Spirit, fill us with light. Give us the strength to understand and eyes to see. Teach us to walk the soft earth as relatives to all that live.

Help us, for without you we are nothing.

—From a Dakota Indian prayer

Days of Birth and Naming

A child is born. A new life begins.

A new person lies in his mother's arms, frail and small and helpless and without a name. The pain of birth is past, and now is the time for joy and thankfulness.

The baby is like a flower unopened, its colored petals hidden in the bud. How will the flower unfold? What will life hold for the child, and what will he show himself to be? How can he be protected against dangers, seen and unseen, and prepared for what he must face in the future when he is grown?

All over the world people have pondered on these things, even while they rejoiced at the birth of a baby and the beginning of a new life. Through the centuries they have found their own ways to protect the newborn child, to welcome him into his family or

11

his tribe, and to give him the blessing of his people's faith.

In many lands the old ceremonies surrounding the birth of a child are dying out, their meaning forgotten. Even in remote villages, hidden in jungles or in high mountain valleys, people are learning new ways to care for their newborn children. Those who move to cities and give up the old village life often leave behind them the customs and ideas of their ancestors. But almost everywhere throughout the world the naming of the child is still the great landmark of his life's beginning.

In Africa the nameless little one in the mother's arms is hardly thought of as a human being. Only when the baby has a name can he or she become a person, a full member of the family, ready to begin the adventure of living.

In the deep forests of Gabon in tropical West Africa the Pygmies sing with joy at a baby's birth and naming.

The mother sings the birth-song, telling of her own private joy, her heart taking flight like a bird under the great forest trees. In the song of praise and gladness at the baby's naming the people wish that the child may live long and be beautiful, and his name is proclaimed for all to hear.

Then the new baby is laid on the ground outside his family's little hut of leaves and branches. The father dances to the beat of a drum, and the family celebrates the holiness and mystery of birth. Joy gives way to reverence and wonder as they sing of the coming of new life into the world. The child is like the good fruit of a tree; his birth is like the dawning of bright day after the blackness of the night.

It is a far cry from the forest camps of the Pygmy hunters to the farming villages and modern cities of West Africa, but here, too, the beginning of life is marked by a special ceremony—the "outdooring." This old custom has not been forgotten, even in cities, and when people from West Africa go to live abroad, they still hold parties for the outdooring of their children.

In Ghana the baby is eight days old at his out-dooring. His mother carries him out of the house for the first time into the fresh air and sunshine. Family and friends are invited to see him and sometimes to bring him presents.

The Ghanaian baby will be given several names. One of them always tells the day of the week on which he was born. If a little boy is born on a Friday, his name has to be Kofi. His brother, born on Tuesday, is Kobla, while his sister—a Sunday child—is Awushi.

Among the Masai people in Kenya, on the other side of the great continent of Africa, cattle are the witnesses of the baby's naming.

The Masai still hold proudly to their old traditions and ways of living, as they wander over the grasslands with their herds. All their wealth is in the long-horned cattle, and every boy of the tribe must be prepared from babyhood to love and care for his animals and to guard them with his life.

No other tribe, say the Masai people, has the right to own cattle, "for God in olden days gave us all the cattle upon the earth."

The Masai child is born in his mother's hut, a tiny round-topped house of woven branches plastered with mud and cow dung. The women of the village are the first to see the baby. As soon as they hear of the birth, they come to the hut with gourds of fresh milk for the mother. Then a sheep is killed and roasted over a fire outside the doorway, and two women bring in the meat. All of them take a slice, and as they eat they sing.

"Hail the day on which this child was born.
Oh joy!
Let us all sing and praise her
That she gave birth to a son
For whom she longed.
Greet this day with joy.
Our hearts are glad."

To celebrate the naming of the Masai child the father makes the greatest sacrifice he can. He kills and roasts a perfect black bullock from his herd— a noble beast with scarcely a spot of white or brown— and invites the family and neighbors to share the meat.

The naming is in the evening of that day, when the mother takes the new baby on her back and goes down to milk the cows in their thorn enclosure. Her husband is waiting for her there with three of the village elders. Between them, the men have decided upon a name and they speak it to the mother as she stands among the cattle with the baby in her arms. The path of the child's life as a herder of cattle is already laid out before him under the evening sky.

If one of the father's cows has recently calved, her calf may be given the same name as the child so that boy and calf may grow up together as brothers.

Shouts of joy, and sometimes the firing of rifles, greet the birth of a baby in Ethiopia—five shouts for a boy and three for a girl.

In the homeland of the Amharic people, the high hilly country at the heart of Ethiopia, the baby is born in a neat round *tukul* house with a pointed thatched roof and walls of pink mud. The setting of his village, with its fields of grain and vegetables, may be a mountain valley, a flat-topped hill or a wide rolling plateau where cattle graze. The village church, round like the houses and roofed with iron or smooth dark thatch, is half hidden in a little grove of trees. The Amharic people are Christians of the Coptic Church. For their babies baptism is the great event of life's beginning.

As soon as the child is born, the women who

16

have helped at the birth sit down in the mother's house to a meal of hot porridge spiced with red pepper, and all who come to visit are invited to join them. Friends and relations bring gifts—a cow and her calf or perhaps a sheep, some fresh-baked bread or a dish of cooked chicken.

"Congratulations that Saint Mary saved you!" they call out to the mother, and she answers them from her bed behind a curtain: "May the Virgin Mary keep you!"

Until the baby is baptized he must never be left alone. A sickle, a chain or some other piece of iron is kept always near him, for the devil is afraid of iron. The ceremony of "going outside" happens when the baby is fifteen or twenty days old. His mother carries him out of the house for the first time, with a man or boy walking ahead, knife in hand, to scare off evil spirits. The mother sits happily in the sun for a while and then invites friends and family indoors to another meal of the special birthday porridge.

When a boy is forty days old and a girl eighty days, the time has come for baptism. The mother and father choose a godparent for their child—a woman for a girl and a man for a boy. On the day of baptism, when the parents and godparent take the new baby to the church, the father carries a pot of water, the godparent brings a length of clean white muslin, and the mother has a thin cord called the *matab* that she has made from twisted threads.

If several babies are ready for baptism at the same time, a little crowd of parents will be waiting in the enclosure around the church for the appearance of the priest and deacon in their white turbans and dark silk cloaks. The deacon leads the way with a lighted taper; the priest bears a beautiful silver cross and an incense burner, and behind him come a second priest and deacon as assistants.

The head priest blesses the *matab* of each baby, dipping the cords in a basin of holy water. Then the godparent gives the baby to the deacon who holds him up and turns him to north, south, east and west, while the priest proclaims the child's name. A second naming comes with the baptism by sprinkling with holy water, and the godparent takes the baby's hand and swears to treat him like a child of his own. The name is spoken for a third time as the priest ties the *matab* around the neck of the little one. This is the sign that he is a Christian.

At last, wrapped in the white muslin, the child is carried into the church. The assistant priest anoints him and names him for a fourth time, while the head priest disappears into the Holy of Holies at the center of the church to prepare for the Eucharist, the Holy Communion service. Before the babies are carried home, each one is given a drop of holy water and a little piece of the consecrated bread.

The baby's Christian name, given at baptism, is chosen by the priest, according to the saint's day or holy day when the baptism is held. The child may be called Gebre Mariam, meaning "Servant of Mary," Haile Meskal, "Power of the Cross," or perhaps Gebre Medhin, "Servant of the Saviour." The baby's "world

name" is the parents' choice and shows their love and pride. A son may be named Ubye or Tesfaye, the Amharic words for "Beauty" and "Hope," and a daughter, Zawditu, "Crown."

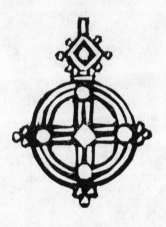

The Galla People in the southern part of Ethiopia speak a different language from the Amhara and many of them are of Moslem faith. When a Galla baby is born, the men of the family sometimes gather together to recite verses from the Koran, the Moslem holy book. They leave the women to give the joyful shouts of *Illil-illil-ill!* that tell the whole village that a child has come into the world.

On the baby's fifth day a sheep or a goat is slaughtered and guests are invited to eat a special dish of coffee beans toasted with butter. This is "Medicine-cutting Day," when the women of the family and their neighbors go out to the woods to cut green branches and gather herbs. These are boiled in a pot and the mother and baby washed in the herb-scented water while the women dance and sing. After

20

they have all eaten a good meal, the oldest woman prays that God will make the baby grow strong, and they chant a song of many verses, wishing the mother long life and a big family of children.

The fortieth day of the Galla baby is the greatest occasion of all. Mother and child are dressed in new clothes. If the mother has given birth in her parents' house, as she does when the baby is her first, she now returns to the home of her husband. He has killed a sheep in readiness and spilled its blood at the gate. The mother must step over the blood and carry the baby around the house, passing through the spicy smoke of incense.

Then, if the child is a boy, he is circumcised. Chief among the people invited for this ceremony are the two *gala*, an older man and a young one, good friends of the parents. They act as godfathers to the child, and if they are wealthy, they bring him a generous gift of money.

The seventh day is an important one for babies born in the Moslem countries of North Africa along the Mediterranean shore. In Libya the child is named on the seventh day, and there is a feast with singing and dancing, while in Algeria, this is the day when the baby can be seen by admiring friends and relatives. He is carried in triumph through every room of the house, followed by girls with bowls of smoking incense to protect the little one from the "Evil Eye."

The seventh-day procession is an old custom in Egypt, too. A string of children dances ahead of the baby with flowers and lighted candles, and as they dance they sing:

> "Birgalatak, Birgalatak,
> Golden ear-rings brightly dangling,
> O God bless him, may he grow up
> And run hither, and play thither
> Up and down the house all over.
> Birgalatak, Birgalatak!"

The baby in an Egyptian village is washed for the first time on his seventh day, just before he is named. The baby's father is probably a farmer, working hard in the fields of grain and cotton and sugarcane beside the Nile. Home is a flat-topped house of brown, sun-dried mud, the color of the earth that gives the people their food. The whole life of the little one, boy or girl, will be bound to the soil and the life of growing things. A small bag of seeds and salt—samples of the fruits of the earth—is sometimes hung around the baby's neck on his seventh day, while his father buries a similar bag in the field, hoping for rich harvests to come.

Before the baby's naming, according to another village tradition, three kinds of grain should be brought into the house in three rush baskets. The little one is laid in a farmer's sieve and the grain poured in around him, and baby and grain are shaken together. The midwife, who has helped at the birth, wraps up the child and sprinkles him with a little more grain before she washes him with water from a painted jug. Then he is given a name. This may be chosen by taking four candles and writing on each one a different name, such as Ibrahim, Ahmed, Harkuf or Uni. The candles are lit and allowed to burn down, and the one that burns the longest bears the chosen name.

In the land of Lebanon, where villages of red-tiled houses cling to the mountainsides like swallows' nests, the birth of a boy was greeted in the old days by the thumping of a drum and the piping of reedy flutes.

As the music filled the village streets and echoed down the terraced fields on the flanks of the mountain, neighbors would hurry to the house of the birth to shower blessings on the child and bring gifts of food and money. All would be served a festive dish of spiced rice pudding called *moghlie*. For a birth in a Christian family friends would light a candle in the church to show their thankfulness.

Nowadays a baby son may still have a noisier welcome than a daughter, but the Lebanese people love their daughters just as dearly. A daughter is looked on as "the flower of the house," and the names of girls reflect their parents' love. Azeezi and Habibi are the Arabic words for "Precious" and "Sweetheart"; Hisn means "Beauty," and Farha, "Joy." In the hope that their sons will grow up with brave, manly qualities, parents may name them Mansour, meaning "Victorious," or Asad, "Lion." In Christian families, boys and girls are given the names of saints.

Grandparents are devoted to their grandchildren. When the village baby goes on his first outing at the age of forty days, he is taken to see his grandparents first of all. The eldest son of a family is generally called after his grandfather, and his proud parents will give up their own names and take the name of their son. If he is called Salim, his mother and father will be known as Imm Salim and Abou Salim for the rest of their lives.

We find a similar custom in Sicily, probably carried there centuries ago by the conquering Arabs. In a Sicilian folksong a father celebrates the birth and naming of his first son:

"From this hour his name will be Turiddu,
My wife, Lucia, will also be known as Turiddu,
And when anyone calls 'Turiddu, Turiddu,'
My wife and my son will come running!"

In Sicily people say that a child born on Friday will be brave and strong and lucky, but almost everywhere in Italy Friday is thought to be a very bad day for a birth. The most fortunate children are born on one of the great feast days of the Church—Christmas, Epiphany or Easter.

Although most parents are happiest when the baby is a boy, there is an old saying in the region of Venice that in the best families the girls are always born before the men. The Tuscans take a severely practical view of the matter. "A man is lucky," they say, "if his first child is a girl, because later on she can help to raise the sons!"

Son or daughter, the new baby in Italy must be christened after a week or two. If the mother follows tradition and stays at home for forty days, she takes no part in the ceremony. The godparents, chosen long before the child was born, are all-important, and their ties with the godchild will be strong as long as they live.

Rousing band music, and even the firing of guns, herald the start of the proud procession along the village streets to the church. The baby, in a white christening gown, is carried by the midwife or a grandparent, and the father and godparents march behind them, all dressed in their best.

In the short ceremony the baby is baptized with holy water and named by the priest. The little one may be given several names, but one of them should be the name of the saint on whose feastday he was born. Little Anna or baby Giorgio will then be under the special protection of Saint Anne or Saint George. The parents hope that just to bear the name of a saint will help the children to live good lives.

When the christening party comes out of the church, friends are waiting to pelt them with sugar candy, peas and beans. Homecoming is a triumphal progress, followed by a tremendous family feast and all the hurly-burly of music and dancing.

The solemn meaning of baptism is remembered in an old custom of village people in the northern

27

province of Veneto. There the newborn child is hurried away to the church for baptism as soon as he has been washed. The door of the house is locked behind him, and when the midwife returns with the baby, she cannot enter the house until the mother hears that the child has been baptized. Then the door is unbolted and flung wide.

"Now that Christ has entered into him," the mother says, "the little one may come in."

In Serbian villages of Yugoslavia the people belong to the Greek Orthodox Church, and a Serbian baby is ten days old when his father and godfather take him to the priest to be christened.

The godfather, called the *kum*, is loved and respected by the parents of the new baby. He will be godfather to all their children. When he dies, he will pass on his position to his son so that the two families will be bound together for generations to come. The *kum* may live in a distant village and travel many miles over the rolling hills, on foot or horseback, to attend the christening. In winter the land will be deep in snow, but in springtime the red-roofed villages sit in bowers of white plum blossom, and the hills are green with grass and new crops.

The *kum* must bring with him a flannel christening robe for the baby, and he also has the duty of deciding on the child's name. Whatever his choice— perhaps Branislav for a boy or Dasenka for a girl—the parents must accept it without question.

When the baby is taken to the priest's house for the christening, it is the godfather who speaks the name as the priest pours water over the naked child. A lock of the baby's hair is cut and rolled into a ball with wax from one of the candles. Then the priest and the two men walk three times around the table with chanting and the swinging of a smoking censer. Finally, the priest makes the sign of the cross over the baby and touches him several times with a crucifix, and the godfather spits lightly to chase away the devil.

Back at the house the baby is on display in the big kitchen, close to the warm stove if it is wintertime. Neighbors and relatives come to admire him and to bring presents, and the baby's grandfather plays host at a fine feast of meat stew, wine and plum brandy, with the *kum* as the guest of honor.

In the country villages of France the birth of a baby is often announced by the joyful pealing of churchbells. The neighbors can tell at once whether it is a boy or a girl, for before the beginning of each tumbling peal a single bell is rung alone—three strokes for a boy and two for a girl. The baby's godfather pays the bellringers. If he is rich and generous, the bells may ring for a whole week!

Whether the child is born in a gray fishing village on the rocky coast of Brittany, in the soft green countryside of the Loire Valley or in the hot sunshine of Provence, he or she is beautifully dressed for the christening. The white robe, rich with embroidery and lace, is so long that it sweeps the ground as the child lies in the godmother's arms. On the baby's head is a square white cap called the *aubette*, with a lacy hood pulled over it. The *aubette* is carefully passed down in the family and used for generations of babies on this first ceremony of their lives.

In the countries of Latin America too, baptism is the great event of the baby's early days.

The child in a Mexican village is baptized as soon as possible after his birth, so that if he should die he will fly up to heaven as a little angel. He is named according to the saint's day on which he was born, but among the Indians of Mexico the real name of the child may be kept secret and a nickname used instead. A sorcerer who found out the child's name could too easily cast a spell on him.

When the Spaniards came to Mexico and converted the Indian tribes to Christianity, the Maya Indians already had a ceremony of their own, resembling baptism, in which the baby was named by a priest. The ancient Maya worshipped time and made gods of the passing days, and relics of this old religion still live on. The Maya believe that a child should be born on a "good day." If he comes on the sixteenth day of the month the whole family is plunged in deep distress, fearing the child will die.

32

Another survival from the ancient past is the Mayan *hetzmek* ceremony. This happens when a baby girl is three months old and a boy four. It marks the first time that the baby is carried astride the hip instead of in a shawl on the mother's back. Godparents, specially chosen for the *hetzmek,* gather with the baby's family around the household shrine—a table set with flowers, candles and small crosses. Food offerings are put on the table for the ceremony, and tools and implements, usually nine in number, are arranged on the floor. For a boy baby there will be the tools of the farmer—a machete, axe, hammer and iron-tipped planting-stick, and perhaps a book as well. A girl will have needle, thread and pins, a *mano* for grinding corn on the stone *metate,* and an iron griddle for baking *tortillas.*

The godmother takes the child in her arms and kneels to pray. Then she puts the baby on her left hip, holding him with her left arm, and goes around the room picking up the tools. One by one, she puts them in the baby's hand and explains how he must use them when he is older. Finally, she goes to the table and gives the child a taste of the various foods, which are symbolic of the qualities he will need in his life. A mouthful of coarse, rough food is to teach the child to endure hardship without complaining; eggs are symbols of understanding, while *pinole,* a powder of toasted corn, is supposed to produce good memory.

Afterwards, the godmother will take the baby to visit the neighbors. He will ride on her hip, as all

33

Maya children are carried until they can walk on their own. Then the whole village will know that he has passed another stage in growing up.

Among the city people of Mexico, as well as the villagers, the baby's fortieth day brings the *sacamisa,* when the mother and godparents take the child to church for Mass. If the godparents have enough money, they buy new clothes for the baby and pay for a special Mass to be celebrated. The priest welcomes the party at the church door and blesses them with holy water. As they follow him up the aisle, the women hold onto the hem of his cape. By bringing the little one to the service they are commemorating the Jewish ceremony performed by the parents of Jesus, when they presented their son in the Temple of Jerusalem.

While Christians take their children to church for protection and blessing during the dangerous days of babyhood, parents of Buddhist faith seek advice and offer prayers in the temples. In Buddhist Thailand, far across the Pacific from Mexico, parents ask the abbot of their local temple to help them pick out lucky names for their children. Like the Maya Indians, the Thais also have an old traditional ceremony intended to prepare the child for his future.

In a Thai village the baby is born in a thatched house set high off the ground on stilts. He is bathed at once. Sometimes there is gold and silver jewelry in the bath water, in the hope that the child will be wealthy. A woman of the family may also carry the newborn baby down the wooden ladder from the house and touch his tiny right foot to the ground three times. This will make him grow up firm and steadfast as the earth.

Then the grandparents tie white threads for luck around the necks and wrists of mother and child, and the baby is laid in a basket. No one must admire him for fear that evil spirits will come to do him harm. He may even be called Pig or Toad to deceive the spirits into thinking him ugly and undesirable. Otherwise the baby is simply *noi*, "little one," or *noo*, "little mouse," until a lucky name is chosen, such as Tiger or Fearless for a boy, and for a girl, Refreshing, Silver or Jewel.

Naming may be done at the ceremony of Shaving the Fire-Hair, when the baby's age is a month and a day. The child's head is shaved clean, except for a tuft on the top. The hair is put into a banana-leaf container, lined with a leaf of lotus, the sacred plant of Buddha. Then, like a little boat, the banana-leaf cup is floated away on the water with the words: "We ask for a life of coolness and happiness like the sacred Ganges."

If the family is wealthy, there will be gifts for the baby on this day; holy water will be poured on his head at the hair-cutting ceremony, and monks will sing a chant of victory.

Then comes the ritual of Entering the Cradle. For this, the hanging cradle must first be filled with a variety of symbolic objects. There is a gourd smeared white with flour; a little mortar and pestle for grinding medicines; and four small bags of rice, vegetables, sesame and cottonseed. For a boy baby a notebook and pencil are added, or for a girl, a needle and sewing thread, and last of all, a big tomcat.

Before the cat has time to escape, the cradle is swung to and fro three times. Then the protesting cat is taken out and the child put in, to be swung for three times more. If he is to be named, the name

will be written on a piece of paper and put into the cradle beside him.

All the things in the cradle have a special meaning and bear the family's good wishes, hopes and prayers for the baby. They want a boy to be a good scholar and a girl a good housekeeper. The bags of food stand for prosperity. We find the meaning of the cat, the white gourd and the stone mortar in the words of an old Thai blessing:

"May you be cool as a gourd and heavy as a pumpkin; may you stay at home like the stones of the fireplace, and guard the house like a tomcat."

When a child is born to a Hindu family in India, his early days are rich with religious ceremonies, especially if his family are Brahmins, members of the priestly caste in Hindu society.

Among the Brahmins of Gujerat, in northwestern India, the new baby's twelfth day is the time of name-giving. Relatives of the father and mother come flocking to the house, and everyone is served with a sweetmeat made of millet seed, coconut and sugar.

The baby's aunt—his father's sister—ties scarlet threads to the cradle and around the baby's waist, to ward off the Evil Eye. Then, for the first time, the little one is carried from the room of his birth to the main room of the house, where the floor has been reddened with clay and spread with leaves of the *pipal* tree. He is laid on a red silk sari and four of his brothers and sisters, or other close relatives, take hold of the corners and swing him gently to and fro. As they swing, they sing the naming song, and the aunt joins in with the name.

"Cradle and *pipala* tree and leaves of the same,
Aunt has chosen .... as baby's name."

This is the baby's first name, and the aunt must follow strict rules in choosing it. The beginning letter of the name depends on what stars were shining when the child was born; Indian astrologers say that certain letters are under the influence of certain constellations. The first name must also include the name of one of the gods or the heroes of Hindu legend. The favorites are Krishna, the god who spent his youth as a simple cowherd, and the mighty hero Rama, whose epic fight with demons is known all over India through storytelling, drama and dance.

The baby may be proudly called Ramakrishna. Then his second name will be that of his father, and the third one must be the name of his family.

When a boy is born into a Rajput family in a village of northern India, he is given a noisy welcome. For ten long days there is drumming and joyful singing outside the door of his mother's mudwalled house.

On the first Sunday after his birth, his mother is beautifully dressed in clean clothes and steps into the courtyard from the small dark room where the child was born. The whole household is assembled to greet her. The baby's grandmother is there, with his aunts and their small children, and neighbor women have been invited to join them from the houses down the street. In honor of this day, called *Bahari*, the brown mud wall around the door of the birth room has been painted with designs showing Hindu gods and goddesses. Servants have set out bowls of food and brought bundles of fresh grass as a sign of plenty and prosperity.

After sprinkling the food with water as a blessing, the mother gives it away to the women who painted the designs and brought the grass. She and her guests and family offer a sacrifice of grain and money to the family ancestors.

Putting on the baby's first clothes—a cloth to go around the middle, a little shirt and a cap—is another occasion for celebration, coming when a boy is six days old and a girl five. The women gather in the courtyard to worship the goddess Bahamata, who brings children, and to pay their respects once more to the watchful ancestors.

The baby's naming can happen at any time after the tenth day, which marks the end of the singing and drumming for a newborn boy. The mother chooses the names for her children. Until she has made her decision, a son is called *lala,* meaning "jewel," and a little girl is *lali.*

The cutting of the baby's hair is a solemn event in the first year of the Rajput child. The hair may be offered up at the shrine of the family ancestors, but to make it a really memorable occasion the parents and children may travel for miles on rutted roads by truck or bullock cart to attend a religious festival in a distant town. Then they can offer up the cut hair in a great temple—so different from the tiny chapels of their village gods, and afterwards enjoy the fun of the festival. There will be outdoor stalls selling sticky sweetmeats, bright trinkets of jewelry and gay cloth for dresses and saris. Perhaps the family can afford to buy something as a reminder of the great day, their baby's first adventure into the outside world.

41

"Sleep, child, sleep!
Today is the twenty-fifth day.
Tomorrow morning this child will make
His first visit to the parish-temple.
When I go with him to the temple,
What shall I pray for?
I will pray that through all his life
This child may be healthy and strong."

This old Japanese lullaby looks forward to the first outing of the Japanese baby—the visit to the Shinto shrine.

For those who follow Shinto, the Way of the Gods, this is the baby's naming day, the time when his birth is recorded and he is formally presented to the gods. Nowadays the baby boy is thirty-two days old and the girl one day older when they are dressed in smart new clothes, made by their loving grandmothers, and taken to the shrine in solemn family procession.

A tall and beautiful gateway of cypress-wood, called a *Torii*, leads into the grounds of the shrine. Sacred *sakaki* trees grow there and the pathway is bordered by stone lanterns, the gifts of faithful worshippers. The shrine itself is built on the simple lines of a traditional Japanese house, with great beams of cypress and a steep roof thatched with cypress bark.

The open prayer hall within has no images of gods, for the Shinto gods are spirits whose form cannot be expressed in paint or carving.

In the quiet beauty of the hall, with its smooth polished floor and wooden pillars, the new baby is presented to the priest to be blessed and named. Everyone hopes the name will bring the child good furtune. Perhaps the parents have chosen to call their new son Hideo, meaning "Excellent Boy," or Tadashi, "Righteousness," while little girls can have such lovely names as Kazuko, "Child of Peace," and Megumi, which means "Blessing."

It is a triumphant small procession that leaves the shrine at last and goes on a round of visits to show the baby to their friends and relations. The day ends in joy and feasting.

When the child is three months old, he has a ceremonial feast all to himself. Tiny bowls of rice and soup, fish, pickles and vegetables are arranged before him on a tray with the chopsticks he must learn to use when he is bigger.

Japanese babies are trained early in good manners, and in being clean, quiet and orderly and respectful to their elders. These rules of living were taught by Confucius in China many centuries ago to help men live together in peace and perfect harmony. Confucius said that the home should be the most peaceful place of all.

"Loving union with wife and children
  Is like the music of lutes;
  But it is the accord of brothers
  Which makes the harmony and happiness lasting."

44

Although Japan is a crowded country, with noisy modern cities and millions of bustling people, the Japanese still feel a closeness to nature, reflected in their worship at the simple Shinto shrines, their love of gardens and the out-of-doors and the way they can express in the few words of a *haiku* poem the loveliness of nature. The child, as he is brought to the shrine, is not only presented to the spirits of ancestors and of great warriors and scholars of the past, but to the nature spirits of the land itself—the spirits of mountain and river, forest and rocky shore. He becomes one with the land of his living, and ready to walk in purity in the Way of the Gods.

The Indian tribes of North America, whose ancestors probably came from Asia thousands of years ago, also believed that every human child born into the world had his place among the living creatures of the earth and the great forces of nature. He was a part of all creation, and the life ahead of him was a road.

For the Omaha Indians the life-journey stretched over four hills—infancy, youth, manhood and old age. In their ceremonies for the child at the start of the journey they expressed this idea in rich poetry.

The newborn child was only eight days old when a priest of the tribe would sing this prayer for him at the doorway of the tent:

"Ho! Ye Sun, Moon, Stars, all ye that move in the
            heavens,
      I bid you hear me!
  Into your midst has come a new life.
      Consent ye, I implore!
  Make its path smooth, that it may reach the
            brow of the first hill!

"Ho! Ye Winds, Clouds, Rain, Mist, all ye that
            move in the air,
      I bid you hear me!
  Into your midst has come a new life.
      Consent ye, I implore!
  Make its path smooth, that it may reach the
            brow of the second hill!

"Ho! Ye Hills, Valleys, Rivers, Lakes, Trees,
            Grasses, all ye of the earth,
      I bid you hear me!
  Into your midst has come a new life.
      Consent ye, I implore!
  Make its path smooth, that it may reach the
            brow of the third hill!

"Ho! Ye Birds, great and small, that fly in the air,
  Ho! Ye Animals, great and small, that dwell in
            the forest,

Ho! Ye Insects that creep among the grasses
and burrow in the ground—
I bid you hear me!
Into your midst has come a new life.
Consent ye, I implore!
Make its path smooth, that it may reach the
brow of the fourth hill!

"Ho! All ye of the heavens, all ye of the air, all
ye of the earth:
I bid you all to hear me!
Into your midst has come a new life.
Consent ye, consent ye all, I implore!
Make its path smooth—then shall it travel beyond
the four hills!"

When Omaha children were old enough to walk, boys and girls went through the ceremony of "Turning the Child," which made them full members of the tribe. Their baby names were then cast away and new names proclaimed, and new moccasins were put on their feet to prepare them for the long journey ahead.

Spring was the season for "Turning the Child." The grass was greening and the birds were in full song when the herald of the tribe announced the time of the ceremony. Parents brought their children, boys and girls of three and four years old. They gathered near a big tent facing eastward, where a priest waited beside a fire.

While a crowd of people watched, the first mother would lead her child to the tent and say to the priest: "Venerable man! I desire my child to wear moccasins."

Then the child entered the tent alone, carrying

his new moccasins, and the mother gave a gift to the priest. "I desire my child to walk longer on the earth," she said. "I desire him to be content with the light of many days. We seek your protection; we hold to you for strength."

The priest then spoke to the child of his life's end, "You shall reach the fourth hill sighing; you shall be bowed over; you shall have wrinkles; your staff shall bend under your weight. I speak to you that you may be strong." He put his hand on the child's shoulder. "What you have brought me shall not be lost to you; you shall live long and enjoy many possessions; your eyes shall be satisfied with many good things."

Then the priest spoke with the voice of the spring thunder: "I am a powerful being; I breathe from my lips over you." And he addressed the winds:

"Ye four, come hither and stand, near shall ye stand
In four groups shall ye stand
Here shall ye stand, in this place stand!"

The priest faced the child to the east and lifted him onto the stone, the emblem of long life, which was placed east of the fire. He turned the child around from left to right, making him face south, west, north and east again, while singing a song to the winds that would strengthen the child to face the trials to come:

"Turned by the winds goes the one I send yonder;
Yonder he goes who is whirled by the winds;
Goes, where the four hills of life and the four
winds are standing;
There, in the midst of the winds do I send him,
Into the midst of the winds, standing there."

Then the new moccasins were put on the child's
feet for his life-journey, while the priest sang again:

"Here unto you has been spoken the truth;
Because of this truth you shall stand.
Here, declared is the truth.
Here in this place has been shown you the truth.
Therefore, arise! go forth in its strength!"

At the last words the child took four steps, the
beginning of his life-journey. Then his new name was
announced, and the priest cried out in a loud voice
the final words:

"Ye hills, ye grass, ye trees, ye creeping things
both great and small,
I bid you hear!
This child has thrown away its baby name. Ho!"

Celebrating
Birthdays

The most joyful of all festivals are birthdays. When people wish each other "Merry Christmas!" or sprinkle the image of Buddha with sweet tea, when they toss a shower of grain at the shrine of the baby Krishna or rejoice for nine days at the birth of the Prophet, all are celebrating birthdays—the most famous birthdays in the world.

The birthday of Buddha is a springtime festival, called the Flower Festival in Japan. Although Buddha was the son of a king, he was not born in his father's palace but in the open air, under a flowering tree. His mother was on a journey to visit her people, carried in a golden palanquin with a retinue of many servants. She gave birth to her son in a grove of blossoming *sal*-trees by the wayside, where the air was filled with birdsong and the humming of multitudes of bees.

51

The story tells how four angels received the newborn baby in a golden net, and four more took him upon a rug of the softest black antelope skin. When at last the servants of the queen placed the baby on the ground, he stood erect, walked forward seven strides and cried in a noble voice: "The Chief am I in all the world."

In the big cities of Japan processions of thousands of children march to the Buddhist temples on the day of the Flower Festival, dressed in their brightest clothes and bearing lotus blossoms. In each temple a little figure of the child Buddha stands in a flowery shrine, and a metal basin is filled with sweet tea, made from leaves of hydrangea. All who come to worship pour tea over the statue from a ladle, remembering the miraculous story of the birth, when showers of tea fell in a sweet rain from heaven.

Japanese children have their own birthday festivals, too. These used always to take place on January first, when everyone in the country added a year to his age, but nowadays, birthday parties more often come on the date of one's own birth, as they do in the West.

A singing game called *Pass Through This Gate* is a favorite on children's birthdays. It tells of a visit

to a Shinto shrine dedicated to Tenjin, the God of
Writing. Two children make an arch with their arms
to represent the tall *Torii* gate of the shrine, and
others line up to pass through. The song is a dialogue,
with alternate lines sung by the gate and the visitors
to the shrine.

"Pass through this gate if you wish;"

"What is this lane, tell us what's this
little lane?"

"This lane belongs to Tenjin, Tenjin God."

"Let us pass, we pray you, let us pass!"

"You cannot pass unless some business brings
you here."

"We have wishing cards for Pippa's seventh
birthday."

Then comes a solemn warning from the gate:

"Going through this gate is peaceful,
But when you return, watch out!
The way is full of danger,
You'll be frightened, we've no doubt.
Take warning if you wish to pass.
Be careful, but pass if you wish."

The visitors go peacefully under the arch on
their way to the shrine, but when they try to come
back, the arch springs to life and pounces on them as
they scuttle through.

In Korea the most important birthdays in a person's life are the first and the sixty-first! The first birthday celebration is a fortune-telling party, an old custom that was born in China and spread to Korea, Japan and Vietnam.

The baby is dressed for the occasion in new clothes of traditional Korean style. A little girl wears a skirt of peach-colored silk and a yellow coat with wide sleeves decorated with contrasting bands. A little boy has blue trousers, a peach-colored coat with banded sleeves and a dark waistcoat fastened with three red buttons. On his head is a black hat that has two broad black ribbons hanging down the back.

The baby is formally introduced to family and friends, with polite ceremonial bowing, and then he is put before a table spread with food. There are bowls of rice and of pungent *kimchi* pickles and plates of sticky rice-cakes. There are also coins and lengths of thread, notebook and pencil and—for a baby girl—a sewing kit. Everything has a meaning for the baby's future, and the family and guests watch eagerly to see what things he will pick up. The threads mean

54

long life and the money, riches, but everyone is specially pleased if a little boy grasps the pencil, for that means he will be a literary man and have a brilliant future indeed!

Afterwards the guests are served with food and given rice-cakes to take away, and each one leaves the baby a gift of money, discreetly folded in an envelope.

In Thailand the celebration of Buddha's birthday is a solemn and holy festival called *Visakha Buja,* taking place in the month of May. There are evening services in the Buddhist chapels. By the light of the full moon long processions of people make their way to the monasteries, bearing candles and colored lanterns. They bring offerings of food and drink and flowers for the monks, who chant songs and recite the Buddhist scriptures far into the night.

Visakha Buja is not a time for gay music or dancing. On this night the people not only remember the birth of Buddha but his death, and the great turning point of his life, the Enlightenment. It was through the Enlightenment that his message to the world was revealed to him. He then set out to lead others in the Eightfold Path, teaching his followers a doctrine of moderation and gentleness, and of kindness to all living things, both men and beasts.

Of the many legends and stories that have grown up around the life of the young prince who became Buddha, the children love best the tales about animals. Before he was born as a prince, Buddha had walked the earth in animal form, once as a beautiful golden stag, another time as a hare, an elephant or a tiger. Yet even as an animal, he had a gentle, generous heart. He believed that all gifts should be shared, and he would willingly sacrifice his life for others.

Children in Thailand remember the teachings of Buddha on their birthdays, and they celebrate by giving gifts rather than receiving them. Birthday children go to the market where live animals are for sale. They spend their money on chickens, goats, or doves, buying one for each year of life and one for the year to come. But instead of killing the animals for food, the children take them to the temple for the blessing of the priest and then give them the most precious gifts of all—life and freedom.

For Hindus in India, especially children, the birthday of Krishna in the summertime is one of the beloved festivals of the year.

When darkness falls on the eve of the great day, the people of towns and villages hurry to the Hindu temples to hear the priests chanting the story of Krishna's birth. They hear how the god was born as a human baby, a little prince in a splendid palace; and how he was threatened with death at the hands of the demon, Kansa, and spirited away in safety to live with a cowherd in a country village. Krishna grew up to be a hero and to do mighty deeds, but the country people love best the tales of his childhood and youth, spent herding cows and playing his flute under the trees.

The chanting goes on in the temple until the stroke of midnight, the hour of Krishna's birth. Then the doors of the inner shrine are thrown open, showing the image of the Baby Krishna in his cradle. All the crowd bursts out with a roar of "Victory!"

The figure of the infant god is bathed in milk, curds, butter, honey and sugar; and the people hold out their hands to receive a few drops of the precious nectar that has washed him. In towns, the statue of Krishna is paraded through the streets in a triumphal torchlight procession.

On the following day the people throng the great fairs held at this holy season. There is music and storytelling, and children give plays about Krishna's life, his love of fun and his tricks and sport among the milkmaids. In Bombay, boys dress up as Krishna. While the spectators squirt them with water, they struggle up a tall greased pole to reach a pot of yoghurt perched on the top. People remember that yoghurt was Krishna's favorite food, and all kinds of foods made from milk are served and enjoyed at his festival.

Hindu children of well-to-do families celebrate their own birthdays, but only until they are sixteen years old. After that, they must put away such childish things.

A private birthday, like Krishna's festival, is first of all a time for worship. The birthday boy or girl rises early to dress in new clothes and go to Mother and Father for their blessing. Then there are prayers to be said at the *Puja,* the family shrine in a quiet corner of the house. Pictures of gods and goddesses hang on the wall. Prominent among them is

the kindly Ganesha, the elephant-headed god of good fortune and new beginnings, a particular favorite of children.

Soon, the family is on the way to the temple with an offering of flowers. The child kneels before the priest, bowing low to the ground in humility, and the priest marks the child's brow with a spot of red or black, a sign that the prayer for a birthday blessing will be answered by the gods.

When the family goes home to breakfast, the birthday child has a whole day's holiday from school. Usually, friends and relatives are invited to midday dinner, with games and present-giving afterwards, but sometimes a child of rich parents will give a party instead for orphans who have no family. The Hindus, like the followers of Buddha, believe that a birthday should be a time for sharing and for remembering those in need.

The great birthday celebration in the Moslem world is the festival called *Mulud*, commemorating the birth of Muhammad.

In Pakistan this is a national holiday with huge parades, marching bands playing and processions of Boy Scouts and Girl Guides. The city streets echo with the holy words of the Koran, as men riding about on trucks recite passages of scripture through loudspeakers. Food is given away to the poor and hungry, sermons are preached in mosques, and people meet together in their houses to recite poems in praise of the Prophet and to tell the miraculous stories of his life's beginning.

Mecca in Arabia, where Muhammad was born, is today the holy city for Moslems everywhere, but at the time of the Prophet's birth, the town had little claim to fame and the birthplace was a small humble house. Yet seven thousand angels brought heavenly dew in a golden ewer for the mother to wash the baby, and all the living creatures of earth and air and water greeted his coming with joy. Even the earth itself rejoiced, and the mountains and the green growing things cried out the great creed that was to be the foundation of the Moslem faith: "There is no god but Allah, and Muhammad is his prophet!"

In Indonesia almost the whole month of the Prophet's birth, the third month of the Moslem calendar, is taken up with the celebrations. In the city of Jogjakarta in Java the festivities start on the sixth day of the month with the opening of a fair, announced by the playing of *gamelan* orchestras in the courtyards of the mosques. People gather at the mosques to listen to the life story of Muhammad and to join in the singing of songs of praise. There is abundant blessing, they believe, in taking part in these ceremonies; and the festival is a good time for starting on important new work, from building a house to knotting a new fishing net.

In Egypt the boom of cannon at sunrise proclaims the day of the birth. Throughout the lands of the Middle East it is a time of prayer and praise and feasting, while at night the domes and minarets of mosques are outlined in hundreds of colored lights.

Private birthdays in this part of the world usually go by unnoticed, except in families who follow Western ways of living. In Iran little children may be crowned with a gold-paper birthday crown and enjoy

presents at home and in school. Boys and girls in the modern cities of Lebanon often celebrate their birthdays as children do in the United States, with presents and a party and a big birthday cake.

Among the Christian people of Lebanon, as in all countries where children are named after saints, the birthday celebration usually comes on the name day, the feast of the child's patron saint. Friends may be invited to a name day party for little Catherine or young James, but the day should begin with worship in the church at the special service in honor of Saint Catherine or Saint James.

When American children sing "Happy birthday to you!" and sit down to feast on birthday cake, they are following an old German custom. The idea of children's birthday parties with present-giving is said to have come from Germany, and a clever German cook invented the *Geburtstagtorten,* a wonderful birthday cake. It has layers of jam inside and sugary icing on top, decorated with fruits and nuts and little figures; and candles are set around the cake for the

64

child to blow out in one puff and make his solemn wish.

In South Germany a small quiet party is held on the child's name day, and the cakes are different. One may have a simple *Gugelhupf* or a rich *Gesundheitkuchen,* baked in a fancy-shaped mold. The guests bring flowers rather than presents, and the glory of the day is that the child is the center of attention and concern and can do whatever he likes. If a child in Munich celebrates his name day in May, he is given lifelike beetles made of chocolate, for this is the season when children catch the big brown "May beetles" on the flowering horsechestnut trees.

In Holland the remembering of birthdays is a serious matter, even after children have grown up. People keep detailed lists of the birthday dates of their friends so that presents and cards can be sent at the proper times. There are elaborate birthday parties and special songs of good wishes for the birthday girl or boy:

> *"Lang zal ze leven*
> *Lang zal ze leven*
> *Lang zal ze leven in de gloria,*
> *In de gloria, in de gloria!"*
> "Long may he live in happiness!"

Presents and parties do not always go with birthdays, and for many children in Europe there are no birthday festivities at all, but everyone can join in the celebration of Christmas, the birthday of Christ.

People in each country have their own Christmas customs and legends, and their own ways of celebrating the feast. Preparations begin weeks before the Day. "Stir-up Sunday," the Sunday before Advent, is remembered as the traditional day for housewives in England to mix and steam their rich plum puddings for Christmas dinner. Presents must be bought, Christmas trees trimmed and rooms decorated with holly and mistletoe and sparkling tinsel.

In houses and churches little carved or modeled figures are arranged in the scene of Christ's nativity in the stable at Bethlehem. Under the thatched roof of the stable the baby lies on the hay in the manger. Mary, his mother kneels beside him, Joseph stands near with the gentle ox and ass and sheep, and the shepherds come in from the fields to give their worship to the Holy Child. The story tells how angels sang that night, as angels rejoiced at the birth of

66

Muhammad and of Buddha. But the heavenly music was unheard by the great ones of the world. Only the shepherds heard the angels' song and came to find the Prince of Peace, homeless as any beggar's child, poor as they were themselves. In the words of the old Medieval carol:

"He came all so still
Where His mother was,
As dew in April
That falleth on the grass.

He came all so still
Where His mother lay
As dew in April
That falleth on the spray."

Wherever Christianity has spread throughout the world there is joy at Christmas.

In the Congo people make a pageant of the Christmas story with a whole village taking part. The stable at Bethlehem is a little palm-thatched shelter decorated with flowers, and at the birth of Christ, a real baby is laid in the manger. The shepherds come to see him with a flock of goats, black and spotted, while the Wise Men are gorgeously dressed in bright hot colors and bear their gifts in hollow gourds.

On Christmas morning, when the thudding of a drum calls the people to church, they, too, have gifts for the baby Jesus. No one comes to the service empty-handed. Some people have presents of money, others carry vegetables from their gardens or fruit from their trees, or a wood carving made with their own hands. The service may last for hours of carol-singing, praying and preaching, but the climax is the offering. Then, as the people come down the aisle of the church to leave their gifts and to share what they have with the newborn Child, they are as proud and humble as the Three Wise Men, when they brought their offerings of gold and frankincense and myrrh.

When Christmas comes to Ecuador in South America the people of the mountain villages have already chosen "godparents" for the Christ Child. On Christmas Eve the godparents arrange a nativity scene at their house, with the loveliest figures of Mary and Joseph and the shepherds that they can find, and invite their friends and neighbors to a meal. After Vespers at the church there are fireworks and balloons for the children, and at last, Midnight Mass, the godparents' most glorious hour.

As though it were a baptism ceremony, they proudly hold the Christ Child, who is often a new-born child of the village, chosen to play the part of the Holy Babe. He is theirs to watch over, in the golden light of the candles, until the service is almost ended and the baby must be passed on to the couple who will serve as godparents in the coming year.

In the night hours after church there is dancing and a feast of such special dishes as guinea pig in red pepper sauce. The new godparents are showered with gifts of baked chickens and other rare delicacies. They look forward with awe and wonder to the part they must play when Christ's birthday comes again.

The drama of a Mexican Christmas is in the nine nights of *posadas,* acting out the journey of Mary and Joseph to Bethlehem and their weary search from door to door for lodgings. The *posadas* begin on December sixteenth, and for days beforehand the markets are full of toys and sweets, little clay figures for making nativity scenes, and wonderful piñatas of all shapes and sizes.

The piñata is a pottery jar decorated with colored paper to look like a cock with spread wings, an elephant, a donkey, a ship or anything the maker can think of; and there must be a new piñata for every night of the nine *posadas.*

In towns and cities of Mexico several families will join forces for a *posada,* and after dark they form a procession, all carrying lighted candles. Two children lead the march, bearing between them a little flat litter with clay figures of the Holy Family—Mary on the donkey and Joseph and an angel following behind. The procession moves singing through the darkness from house to house, grownups and children together, until they come to the house where they

71

hope to stop that night. They knock on the door, and when it is opened, they all sing Joseph's plea for lodging:

"In the name of heaven
Give us lodging,
My beloved wife
Can go no further!"

The man of the house sings his refusal and turns away all entreaties until at last Joseph sings:

"My wife is Mary,
The Queen of Heaven,
She is to be mother
Of the Holy Word."

Then the door is flung wide.

"Are you Joseph?
Your wife is Mary?
Enter, travellers,
I did not know you!"

In the house a manger is set up ready for the Christ Child, and everyone kneels before it to pray. There are good things to eat and perhaps a dance, and then all eyes turn to the piñata, hanging from the ceiling. One of the children is blindfolded, whirled around three times and given a stick to smash the piñata. He swipes the stick in all directions while everyone laughs and dances around him in a circle. The whole party may have a try with stick and blind-fold before a well-aimed blow hits the jar with a crash and shatters it and a shower of nuts and sweets comes tumbling down.

For eight nights the procession makes its pilgrimage and smashes a piñata. The ninth and final night is Christmas Eve, when the journey of Mary and Joseph is ended and the Christ Child is born. The visitors bring with them the figures for the nativity scene, and while little children dressed as shepherds stand on either side, two people acting as godparents lay the figure of the baby Jesus in the manger. Then everyone kneels to sing the baby to sleep with a Christmas cradle song.

"A la ru-ru-ru, My Lovely Jesus,
In sweetest slumber now rest, my dearest."

This last *posada* is followed by Midnight Mass. The night is brilliant with fireworks and joyous with the clamor of bells, and everybody goes home at last to enjoy a big supper.

For the village people of Mexico the *posadas* are held in church. Boys and girls do shepherd dances to the music of the violin and the rhythmic tapping of sticks, and groups of village dancers come to entertain the baby Jesus lying in the manger. The figure of the baby stays in the church until Epiphany, when the Wise Men bring presents for Mexican children and the wonder of Christmas is ended for another year.

Christ's birthday is a thrilling time for children in Mexico; their own name days pass quietly, and most children must wait until they are grownup before they can have a full-scale name day celebration, with streams of visitors filling the house all day. Traditionally, the festivities start at dawn, when a *mariachi* band wakes the whole neighborhood with splendid music and a lovely *mañanita* is sung under the window of the fortunate person:

> "On the day when you were born
> All the flowers were born.
> On the day when you were born,
> The nightingales were singing.
>
> *Now comes the dawn,*
> *Now we see the light of day.*
>
> Now wake up, my friend,
> See how the dawn has come.
> For the moon I give a peso,
> For the sun one half a peso,
> For my friend Susanita
> My life and my heart.
>
> *Now comes the dawn,*
> *Now we see the light of day!"*

For those children in Mexico and Central America who are lucky enough to have birthday or name day parties, the piñata is always the high point of the occasion. The guests may be specifically invited "to break a piñata." The bigger and more elaborate it is, the better.

In Venezuela the birthday piñata is made of papier maché, instead of being an earthenware pot, and it can be beautifully modeled in the shape of a swan, a castle or a ship. Country children, who cannot make or buy such fancy pinatas, have just as much fun with a gourd or a cardboard box made gay with paper streamers and hung from the branch of a tree. Someone cunningly jiggles the piñata up and down to make it harder to hit. It is a real triumph when the nuts and sweets and fruits come bursting out!

Birthdays are remembered in school in Venezuela, and the children sing for the lucky member of the class. Their song is full of bees and nightingales and moonlight and warm with the good wishes that attend birthdays everywhere:

"Today is your day filled with grace and with light:
 May you celebrate it in honor
 May you celebrate it in joy
 That your heart be made full and run over.

May fortune smile at you
Amidst flowers and music and sweatmeats,
Nectar and hope,
Today, your own day.

May the bees make you offerings of their honey,
And dawn, the gift of its splendour.
Of nightingales receive their song,
And of cherubs their love.

May the moon encircle you with
Pearly fire,
And the stars admire you
From their rainbowed clouds."

Ceremonies of
Growing Up

A birthday is a time of joy, but underneath the laughter and the songs and the present-giving, birthdays have a solemn meaning. The child is a year older, a year closer to the end of childhood and the beginning of a new life as a man or a woman.

All over the world there are special ceremonies performed to mark that new beginning. Young people on the threshold of adulthood are called upon to prove their strength of body and brain, their courage in the face of pain and loneliness. Above all, they must go through a period of hard study and learning, to prepare them for the life that will be theirs. Beyond the practical ways of making a living lie the mysteries of religious faith. Often the gateway to adult life is through learning to take a full part in prayer and worship in the temple or the mosque, the synagogue, church or shrine.

79

Growing up is never easy. The growing person is torn two ways, half wanting to stay young and carefree as a dependent child, half longing to break loose and strike out alone. Although people in tribal societies have a very different life from dwellers in modern cities, they know, and have always known, the difficulties of growing up. Their wise ancestors long ago devised initiation ceremonies in which the children of the tribe could make a clean break with childhood. Afterwards, there would be no looking back. It was as though the children had died and then come alive again as adults. They had been born again.

Until recent years many of these old rituals still survived among the aboriginal people in the wild places of Australia. In the past each tribe throughout the continent had its own ceremony, often long and painful, for initiating boys into manhood. One of the simplest, and perhaps oldest, of these rites belonged to the Kurnai tribe, who lived in Gippsland along the southeastern coast of Australia.

The Kurnai boys chosen for initiation assembled

in the open air. Their mothers stood close behind them, while the older men, who were to be the boys' teachers, came out of the bush in procession. The men were smeared black with charcoal, and strips of white bark were tied around their bodies, heads and limbs. Tall tufts of grass nodded from the bark coronets. Each man carried a bundle of wooden rods.

The men marched around the boys and women and then passed down between them, cutting off the sons from the mothers. Then they tossed their rods into the air and lined up in front of the boys in groups of three. Each group, with loud shouting, lifted a boy three times, as high as they could, with his arms stretched up toward the sky.

Then the boys were led away from the camp of their people to a sacred place in the bush. They lay down on a couch of leaves and were covered over with skins and forbidden to move or speak. From now on, they were told, they were no longer children; they must act like men. The boys fell into a trance-like sleep while the men and women danced around them for hours with monotonous chanted song. At daybreak the men lay down to rest and the women went back to the camp, knowing they would be killed if they heard or saw what was to come. When the boys were uncovered and wakened, they were given men's dress of belt, kilt, armlets and headband, and their serious training began.

The heart of the initiation was the ceremony called "Showing the Grandfather." An hour before sunset the boys were ordered to kneel down, their

81

heads covered with blankets. One instructor knelt before each boy and another stood behind. Then they heard a strange booming sound. Nearer and nearer it came, rising to a mingled roaring and screeching, until at last the blankets were pulled from their heads and a voice commanded the boys three times to look up.

Men stood before them in a semicircle, and the awful sound came from the flat piece of wood that each man was whirling on the end of a cord. These were the sacred bull-roarers, the large deep-toned ones called Man, and the smaller ones, Woman.

Then the Headman told the ancient story of the beginning of the Kurnai people. Long, long ago, in the Dream Time, when the high god, Mungan-Ngaua, walked the earth, two bull-roarers, Man and Woman, were used at the first initiation of the tribe. The Kurnai people were the children of the high god's son, Tundum, and the god himself taught them how to make tools, canoes, nets and all they needed for living. But the secrets of the initiation were betrayed to the women of the tribe. The god was so angry he turned his son and his son's wife into porpoises and destroyed nearly all the people on the earth by fire and raging water. Then he rose into the sky and never returned.

When the boys had heard the story, they were allowed to whirl the sacred bull-roarers with their own hands. After dark they were led slowly through the bush around the camp of their people, sounding the bull-roarers to strike fear in the hearts of the women and children.

The boys were now forbidden to go near their mothers. As children, the boys were dead, yet before they could begin their new life as men they must spend many days with their teachers in the bush. Even as adults they would continue to learn, for initiation was only the beginning of lifelong learning. A man must live to be old in years before he could know all the myths and mysteries of the tribe.

In Africa, too, the awful sound of the bull-roarer was heard at the time of initiation. Its voice might be the voice of the tribal ancestors; or it might represent the roar of lions at night, when small boys crouched in the dark forest and endured a trial of fear, a preparation for the ordeal of circumcision that would make them men.

Among African hunters, such as the Bushmen of the Kalahari Desert or the Pygmies of the Congo forests, a boy becomes a man when he kills his first large animal, proving his skill as a hunter and his fitness to marry and support a family. But in most tribes manhood comes through ceremonies, tests and hard schooling.

Children brought up in the old ways of tribal Africa begin their learning as babies in their mothers' arms. Through songs and lullabies, stories and proverbs, their mothers teach them the names of their ancestors, the history of their people, and the rules of tribal custom and behavior. As soon as little boys can walk, their fathers take them to dig and pull weeds in the fields, and soon the boys are given gardens to care for on their own. Little girls learn from their mothers the women's work of grinding grain and cooking. They look after their baby brothers and sisters and carry loads of firewood and child-size water-pots.

Boys and girls explore the world around them, learning about its plants and animals, its dangers and delights. Every day they are learning, not by sitting in a classroom but by living and doing, by keeping eyes and ears open and storing things in mind and memory, without the help of books. Children of seven or eight years old know nearly all they need to know about making a living according to the way of their people. Then comes initiation.

Boys of the Bira people, forest farmers of the Congo, are initiated when they are between nine and twelve years old. When the players of *makatas*, the sacred musical sticks, come dancing into the village, the boys know their time is near. Soon the priests appear in terrifying spotted masks, with bells on their arms and legs. They dance for a week to the beat of drums and single out the boys for initiation.

The chosen ones are shut up in a dark room.

While the drumming and dancing go on outside, they are told that they are going to die and come alive again.

After several days they are taken away from the village to be circumcised and to begin their learning at a special camp in the forest. With little food or sleep, their bodies daubed with white clay as a sign of death, they work for three months to learn the songs and dances of their people, the proverbs and moral laws handed down to the tribe by the ancestors, and the way to seek the help of the ancestors in time of trouble.

When at last the schooling is over and the boys are led back to the village, they dance a wild dance of triumph. Early next morning they wash off the white clay of death. Then they lie down under a blanket of leaves during the final ceremonies and spring up as though from a grave—men, strong and confident, ready to take their places in the tribe.

Among the Masai people of Kenya initiation comes when boys are in their teens. They are growing in strength and have long been herders and defenders of their fathers' cattle. They know each cow and bullock by its name. Many of the boys, from babyhood, have had their own calves to love and care for. They have cheered the cattle with dancing and song, treated them in sickness and grieved for them in death. The cattle, in return, have provided them with the traditional food of the Masai warrior—fresh milk mixed with warm blood drawn from the necks of bullocks.

At the time of initiation boys from several villages gather at the camp of a medicine man. He separates them into two age-groups. The group of smaller boys is sent home to wait a few more years for initiation. The others begin at once to listen and to learn while the medicine man and the elders in the camp explain the customs and beliefs of their people and, above all, the duties of the warrior.

After three months of this schooling, the boys return to their villages to be circumcised. The father of each boy kills one of his precious bullocks in honor of the event. He calls it the "Animal-to-be-taken-out," because the boy has been taken out of the ranks of children and will soon be moving up to the rank of Young Warrior. The boy's head is shaven, in the fashion of the girls of the tribe, and after his circumcision he wears a long blanket robe. He might be mistaken for a girl if he had not whitened his face with a mask of chalk.

While his hair grows long again, as the hair of a warrior should be, the boy is free to roam about the country with others of his age-group. All their lives the age-mates will be closely knit together, and their loyalty to each other will link up scattered families and help to unite the tribe. Now, in their wanderings,

87

the boys get to know the people, the animals and the land, and store up their knowledge for the future.

After a second initiation, to make them into Young Warriors, the boys go to live in a *manyatta,* a warriors' village. Their duty is to guard the *manyatta,* which has no thorn fence to protect it, and to watch over the nearby cattle camps of their people. The boys practice constantly with club and spear and shield. Soon they will be strong enough to kill a lion single-handed, and in a few years they will achieve the full rank of Man and Warrior.

The old idea of initiation as dying and being reborn runs like a golden thread through the thought and religion of many different peoples. The Hindus of India, whose history, faith and philosophy reach back for hundreds of years, call themselves the Twice-Born. The initiation of the Hindu boy is his second birth,

a spiritual birth called *upanayana,* "the beginning of wisdom."

The ceremony of *upanayana* is only for those who belong to the three highest castes of Hindu society—the Brahmins, who are priests and religious teachers; the Kschatriya, the caste of soldiers and rulers, protectors of the weak; and the Vaisyas, who are farmers, shopkeepers and merchants. A Brahmin boy is usually eight years old when he goes through the ceremony; boys of the other two castes are eleven or twelve.

The young Brahmin is carefully instructed beforehand by a *guru,* a priestly teacher, and an astrologer decides upon an auspicious day for the ceremony, generally in the second quarter of the year. The boy must spend the night before in complete silence. In the morning he takes his place with his parents under a canopy in the courtyard of their house, where a fire is burning. A barber comes forward to cut the boy's nails and shave his head, except for the long lock of hair on the top, and the boy bathes and puts on clean clothes.

Sweet food is brought. For the last time the boy eats with his mother, who knows that after the *upanayana,* her son will be a man, unable to eat with women. The boy also shares food with other boys like himself before he goes alone to sit by the fire with his *guru.*

Then, from the hands of the *guru,* he receives the sacred cord, a white cotton thread of three strands twisted together, the symbol of second birth. He holds the cord between the thumb and smallest finger of each hand while the *guru* recites a prayer for strength, long life and spiritual illumination. At the last words the boy slips the cord over his head and lets it hang from his right shoulder, reaching across his body to the left hip. In this way he will wear the cord all his life, as the sign that he is *dvija*, twice-born, a full member of the religious community of his people.

Now, as he faces his teacher, the man pours water from his own cupped hands into the palms of the boy. Taking the boy's right hand, the *guru* gives him a new name, kept secret and only used on this day. Then the heads of the boy and man are veiled with a silk scarf while the *guru* whispers into his pupil's right ear the holiest of all verses: "Let us meditate on the most excellent light of the Creator; may he guide our intellects."

The boy's right ear is made forever holy after hearing the verse. He must learn to repeat the blessed words every day for the rest of his life. Now he puts wood on the fire and speaks a prayer for help and protection. The *guru* gives him a blessing, the boy bows, and the ceremony is over.

The child has become a man, even though he is only eight years old. That same evening he may perform the ritual of evening prayer, one of the daily duties of a Brahmin. Through prayer and study he must seek always for a deeper understanding of spiritual things, a closer communion with the Creator, the One God, of whom the many gods of temple and shrine are only single aspects.

Each year, as he moves through the stages of his life, the Twice-Born will keep the anniversary of his rebirth and receive forgiveness for a whole year's sins. He sees his life laid out before him in an orderly pattern, going from the first stage, childhood and youth, through the stage of marriage and family to the time when his children will be grown and he can retire from active life and devote himself to meditation and prayer.

In the wisdom of old age he may even attain the fourth stage and become a wandering religious teacher, like his own *guru*. Then he will travel on foot from town to town, resting only in the four-month growing season, because his reverence for the earth's new springing life forbids him to tread it underfoot. Poor in worldly goods but immeasurably rich in spirit, he will be respected by everyone, and one day, in his turn, he will be the teacher of a young boy preparing for second birth and the beginning of wisdom.

In Burma a boy becomes a man in the *Shinbyu* ceremony, when he is initiated into the Buddhist priesthood at the age of twelve or fourteen.

The *Shinbyu* is like a drama, acting out the story of Buddha's Great Renunciation. The boy plays the part of the young prince who fled from his palace and gave up wealth and birthright for a life of lonely meditation until he was granted Enlightenment. Parents in Burma have the duty of arranging for the *Shinbyu* of their sons. Sometimes rich people will provide a ceremony for orphans and boys of poor families, so that all may have the opportunity of walking in the footsteps of Buddha.

The best season for the *Shinbyu* is at the beginning of *Wa*, the Buddhist Lent, which lasts from July to October. The day is chosen according to the boy's horoscope, and invitations sent out to many friends and relatives. In a wealthy family a pavilion is set up in front of the house and a great feast prepared there. The young boy himself, the center of attention, is clad like a prince in gleaming silk, and rides around the town on a white horse for everyone to see him, handsome and proud. A band of musicians goes before him, and his friends dance and sing.

93

When at last he returns to his parents' house, the pomp and glory of the world are flung aside. The Buddhist monks, with their shaven heads and plain yellow robes, are waiting for the boy in the pavilion, where they have received simple gifts of robes, fans and slippers from his family.

The boy takes off his bright turban and clothes of silk; his hair is cut off and his head smoothly shaved. He prostrates himself three times before the monks, begging them to let him enter their Holy Assembly. The abbot of the monastery gives him the yellow robe, and the monks surround him and take him away. Then the family and guests sit down to their feast, followed by a *pwé*, a performance of drama and music that may well go on until dawn.

The next day the boy comes back to visit his home with other monks. He bears a begging bowl as they do, to receive food from the faithful, and his eyes are cast down in humility. He has a new name, for his season in the monastery. His mother treats him no longer as her son but pays him reverence as a holy man.

His duties now are to study and to serve the monks. He is wakened at the first light of dawn by the pounding of a wooden bell. He must go forth each morning to beg for food and must be content with one meal a day. He tries to follow "the middle path . . . which leads to insight, which leads to wisdom, which conduces to calm, to knowledge, to perfect enlightenment, to Nirvana"—the final state of bliss in self-forgetfulness.

94

The monks teach him to be independent in his thinking and not to accept without question what he is told. Enlightenment and Nirvana are not an inheritance of birth but can only be attained through study and meditation. As the boy has reenacted the Great Renunciation, so he can follow Buddha to Enlightenment, for each man has it in himself to become a Buddha.

A week or two in the monastery may be enough for the boy, but if he stays throughout the whole season of *Wa*, his learning in the company of the monks can give him a firm and lasting foundation for right living in the world.

Parents in Thailand also see the goodness of monastic life and teaching for their sons and hold a joyous festival when a boy renounces the world for a season and "takes the yellow robe."

On the eve of his going, a big crowd gathers for a feast and a whole night of music and dance. Only the young man takes no part, sitting silent in the midst of the babble and talk and the sparkling music of the gongs, drums and flutes of the *piphat* orchestra.

The next day his family serves him a meal of the finest food he has ever tasted. Then his head and eyebrows are shaven and he is led to the monastery in a long procession, beautiful with banners, fans and bright umbrellas, moving to the rhythm of drums. When they reach the monastery, the boy's mother takes him into a chapel for a short ceremony admitting him to the community. He begins three months of meditation and prayer, from which he will come forth, like the Burmese boy, with a new maturity of spirit, the beginning of manhood.

In Israel, and in Jewish communities throughout the world, a boy's childhood ends when he is thirteen years old. He then becomes *Bar Mitzvah*, a Son of the Commandment, responsible for a man's religious duties of prayer and fasting and attendance at the synagogue.

By the time the great day arrives, on the Sabbath before his thirteenth birthday, the boy has been

well trained in the faith of his people. He can recite the prayers and read fluently from the Hebrew scriptures. Now his father gives him a full-sized prayer shawl and the *tephillin* that he must wear, as a man, when he says his daily prayers at home.

The *tephillin*, his father tells him, will help in turning his mind and heart toward God and away from the distraction of earthly things. Each of the two narrow strips of black leather has a square box attached containing texts from the Bible written on small pieces of parchment. The boy knows that these are verses from the books of *Exodus* and *Deuteronomy*, proclaiming that the Lord is One and telling of his care for Israel and his deliverance of his Chosen People from slavery in Egypt. One of the *tephillin* must be bound around his left arm, near his heart, and the other to his forehead, near the brain, before he begins to pray.

On that Sabbath Day the boy goes with his family to the synagogue, taking his new prayer shawl with him. The women and girls sit up in the balcony; the boy has a place below with his father and the other men, and he covers his head with the prayer shawl while he prays. Then he puts the shawl around his shoulders, and the service begins with a hymn and the cantor's call to prayer.

The boy watches anxiously when the great scroll of the Torah is carried to the reading desk and opened for the reading of the *Sidrah*, the portion of scripture appointed for the day. The cantor reads the *Sidrah* in seven parts, with a blessing before and after each one. Then comes the moment the boy has waited for. He is called to the desk to read from the Torah himself, in front of all the people.

He must read clearly and without stumbling. He may also be required to chant a passage from the Prophets and recite a short address of his own, in which he thanks his parents and teachers and vows to follow in the ways that they have taught him.

After he returns to his seat, the service goes on as usual, but for the boy the world has changed. People congratulate him as they leave the synagogue. In the old days, when the boy's speech was often a scholarly discourse on the Law, there would be heated discussions and criticisms of what he had said.

Nowadays, the family gives a feast in honor of their son, with friends and relations gathered from far and near. The ceremony of *Bar Mitzvah* is no longer looked upon as the gateway to marriage and family life, as it was in the past. The boy has much growing up still to do, but he has closed the door on childhood, and in his spiritual life he is already a man.

Like the Jewish boy becoming *Bar Mitzvah,* the Hindu putting on the sacred cord and the Buddhist the yellow robe, Christian boys and girls also have a spiritual coming of age.

In many of the churches the time arrives with Confirmation and first Communion. As the young people kneel before the altar at the Confirmation service and the bishop lays his hands on their heads, they renew the vows made at their baptism, when they were first accepted into the company of the faithful. The ceremony of Confirmation leads to Communion. For the first time, with the adults of the congregation, the boys and girls take their full part in the service.

If this important day comes early in life, the little boys in their best suits and girls in white dresses and fluttering veils may be too young for complete understanding of what they are doing. But the first step has been taken. They have attained the beginning of wisdom, and the door is open to them to enter into the deeper mysteries of faith.

101

However young the child may be when he becomes an adult in his spiritual life, his coming of age in the eyes of the world must usually wait until the twenty-first birthday. For many girls in Latin America, though, the fifteenth birthday is the important one. In Brazil and in the Central American countries this brings the wonderful Fifteenth Birthday Party when the girl is introduced into society.

In Mexico the day begins with going to morning Mass, while the household is already in a whirl of preparations for the evening. If the girl's parents are well-to-do, the rooms are decorated with flowers, and by nightfall the patio glows with colored lanterns. The girl is beautiful in her new long evening gown, all ready to dance with her young cousins and the sons of family friends.

Crowds of guests begin to arrive—people young and old, from the newest babies to the oldest grandparents. A *mariachi* band, resplendent in scarlet and gold, tunes up guitars and violins, cellos and horns, and swings into the traditional music of Mexico, while for the young people there may be a modern dance band as well, with tunes from north of the border.

The house is filled with dancing, while servants run to and fro with drinks and snacks, just enough to keep everyone energetic and lively. It is long after midnight before the dancers stop to rest and to enjoy an elegant buffet supper of salads and rich creamy cakes and desserts. When the party breaks up and the last guest has said goodbye, the night is fading into dawn.

The tireless servants, talking and laughing, begin at once to tidy the rooms. The fiesta is over, but the daughter of the house will never forget this night. How different it was from the simple parties of her childhood! More than a party, this was the celebration of her coming of age, the announcement that she is now ready for marriage. She has become a woman, and before many years have passed, she will be a wife and mother.

When her next birthday comes, there may be a *mariachi* band to play a serenade under her window at dawn, as though she were a grown-up person, and there will be real meaning in the words of the old *mañanita* that they sing:

> "These are the Mañanitas,
> That King David sang
> And to the pretty girls
> He sang them thus:
>
> Awake, my love, awake,
> Look, it is already dawn;
> The birds are singing
> And the moon has gone in.
>
> What a lovely morning,
> It looks as if it will rain.
> The morning was the same
> When I began to love you.

If the watchman of the corner
Wished to do me the favour,
He would put out his little lantern
While my love passes by.

And now, yes, Mr. Watchman,
I thank you for your favour,
You may light your little lantern
For my love has passed by."

The growing up of Maya Indian children in Mexico and Guatemala is not a time of fiesta but of greater responsibility and harder work.

In the past, when the Spaniards invaded their country, the Maya still performed an ancient ceremony by which children became adults, boys and girls together. An old man served as godfather for the company of boys and a woman for the girls. A priest gave each child some incense and maize to throw on a brazier in the courtyard where the ceremony took place. Then, with white cloths placed on their heads, the children were blessed by the priest and sprinkled with holy water.

Today the Maya children grow up early, without ceremony, firmly trained from their earliest years to be quiet, industrious and uncomplaining in times of hardship.

The boys, who have handled the tools of farmer and huntsmen at the *hetzmek* ceremony of their babyhood, begin helping their fathers in the fields at six years of age, and in a few years they are skilled farmers. At thirteen they are allowed fields of their own for growing corn and beans and squash. Girls of the same age are given looms for weaving.

Childhood is behind them. The young boy praying to the Holy Saints to send rain for his planted field and the young girl patting out *tortillas* for the midday meal already have the skills that fit them for adult life, for early marriage and the making of a home of their own.

The Navaho Indians of the American Southwest still lead their children into adulthood by a special rite.

At the waning of the year, after the first frosts of winter have come to their desert land, the Navaho perform the long ceremonial chant called the Night Way. On the next to last night of the performance two assistants of the tribal medicine man prepare themselves to conduct the initiation of the children.

The two men wash their hair in yucca suds, dress in kilts and ornaments and whiten their skin with clay. One man puts on the black mask of the Grandfather of the Monsters and the other the white mask of a goddess. Then they make their way to an open place where the chosen boys and girls, between seven and thirteen years old, are already assembled. A fire is burning there, and each child has been covered with a blanket and warned not to look at the gods who will soon be coming. The mothers of the children stand behind them and talk and joke with the company of men on the other side of the fire.

When the two masked gods appear, the first boy, naked except for a loincloth, is led close to the fire. The white-masked god marks the boy's shoulders with sacred cornmeal. At each marking, the black-masked one gives a strange, high-pitched cry. With a bunch of reeds bound together he strikes the marks and hits the boy about the body, crying shrilly before each blow, while the crowd of people burst into laughter if the boy jumps and starts with surprise.

One by one the boys are treated in the same way. Then it is the girls' turn. They are seated on the ground, fully dressed. After their shoulders have been marked with the cornmeal, the black-masked man presses the marks with two ears of corn, one in each hand, wrapped in spruce twigs.

Then the two men take off their masks and lay them down on either side of the fire, and the children can see that they are men indeed and not immortal beings. Each child is given pollen to sprinkle on the masks and to throw at the two men. The terrible mask of the Grandfather of the Monsters is taken up again by the man who had worn it. But instead of wearing the mask himself, he places it carefully on the face of each child in turn so that each may look through the eye-holes and feel no fear.

The children are now bidden to look up and to remember the Holy People, the supernatural beings who created the ancestors of the Navaho and taught them all they needed to know in order to live and to increase in the land. The children are warned to tell no one what they have heard and seen. As children no longer, they bear secrets to be forever hidden from the uninitiated.

The mysterious ceremony prepares the Navaho children to play their parts in tribal life, but many of those who leave the place of their initiation, awed and silent, will soon be living in a world far removed from the ancient ways and deep-rooted traditions of their people.

The young Navahos already know the world of school that seemed at first so strange and rigid. They know what it is like to be called by a fixed, unchangeable name and to sit for many hours in a classroom, where time is measured by the hands of the clock instead of the movement of sun and shadow. In that world a boy's ability to look after his father's sheep in the great desert is of little importance; and old customs and stories and myths, carried in the heart and mind, must give way before the facts of science and history written down on printed pages.

Today, when so many children everywhere spend most of their time in school, the ceremony of graduation has become their initiation rite, prepared for during years of study. The examinations at the end of school are the ordeals they must undergo. The diploma they receive is as real a token of the end of childhood as the tattoo-marks on the chest of the young Pygmy hunter, the sign that he has made his first big kill and so become a man.

Graduation, even from primary school, can be a new birth, a fresh beginning—one of those moments of growing up that is a struggle between looking back at the past and forward to the future.

"My last six years of life in school passed in my head like a film," said a Korean boy, after his graduation from primary school. "Last year I laughed at those graduates who were shedding tears. I mocked them. 'Ha! you are crying like girls!' This year, I had a hard time to keep back my tears."

Yet all over the world the pains of growing are matched by hope and pride and the joy of adventure. Those who are growing up will rise from their sadness as new people, ready to go on with their journey.

The road lies ahead of them, as the Indians saw it long ago—the winding road of the four hills. The way of childhood is past and left behind. Now the boys and girls are travelling into unknown country, their feet shod with new moccasins for the long journey ahead. No one can tell where the way will lead them, but before the end of the journey their strength, their gifts and their spirit will be passed on to a new generation.

Once more, through joy and pain, new life will come into the world. A child will be born. . . .

In beauty may I walk.
All day long may I walk.
Through the returning seasons may I walk. . . .
With beauty may I walk.
With beauty before me, may I walk.
With beauty behind me, may I walk.
With beauty above me, may I walk.
With beauty below me, may I walk.
In old age wandering on a trail of beauty,
    lively, may I walk.
In old age wandering on a trail of beauty,
    living again, may I walk.
It is finished in beauty.
It is finished in beauty.

—From the Navaho Night Chant

Appendix

MUSIC OF BIRTHDAY SONGS

From Egypt

Birgalatak

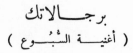

"Bir-ga-la-tak bir-ga-la-tak
halk da-hab fi-wdanatak
Igri héna imshi héna
notté héna wil-âb héna
Ya Rab-bina ya Rab-bina
yik-bar wi yib-a ad-dina

"Birgalatak, Birgalatak
Golden ear-rings brightly dangling
O God bless him, may he grow up
And run hither, and play thither
Up and down the house all over.
Birgalatak Birgalatak."

("Birgalatak" is a made-up word having no meaning.)

Reprinted from *Egyptian Folk Songs*, Cairo, 1958, with permission of the compiler Baheega Sidky Rasheed.

114

From Holland

A Birthday Song

(Lang zal die leven)

Old Dutch Melody

Lang zal die (ze) leven
Lang zal die (ze) leven
Lang zal die (ze) leven in de gloria
In de gloria, in de gloria.

Long may she (he) live,
Long may she (he) live,
Long may she (he) live in happiness,
In happiness, in happiness.

Pass Through This Gate

(Toryanse)

Dramatically

1.
Pass through this
To - ryan - se,

2.
gate if you wish; | What is this lane, tell us | what's this lit-tle lane?
to - ry-an - se. | *Ko - ko-wa do - ko-no* | *ho - so-mi-chi ja?*

1.
This lane— be-longs to | Ten-jin,Ten-jin God | Let us pass, we—
Ten - jin — sa - ma - no | *ho - so-mi-chi ja.* | *Chot-to to sh'te*

1.
pray you, let us pass! | You can - not pass un - less some
Ku - da sha - n - se. | *Go - yo - no na - i - mo - no*

2.
bus-'ness brings you here. | We have wish-ing cards for *(Pip-pa's)
to - o sha - se - nu. | *Ko - no - ko - no na - na-tsu - no*

1.
*(sev-enth) birth-day. Go - ing | through this gate is peace-ful, but when
o - i - wa - i - ni - i, | *o - fu - da - o o - sa - me - ni*

116

you re - turn, watch out.
ma - i - ri - ma - su.

The way is full of dan - ger,
I - ki - wa yo - i yo - i,

You'll be fright-ened, we've no doubt.
Ka - e - ri - wa ko - wa - i,

Take warn-ing if you wish to
Ko - wa - i - na - ga - ra - mo

pass. Be care - ful, but
To - o - rya - n - se,

pass if you wish.
To - rya - n - se.

* Child's name and age.

The game is sung in dialogue as indicated by numbers 1 and 2. Two children form an arch with arms upraised, and sing on 1.

The group passes on 2 under the arch, single file, supposedly going to the shrine. All are allowed to pass freely "going." Then, on their return, the arch-makers try to catch and hold as many as possible; thus the way back is "dangerous" as they dart under the arch trying to avoid being caught.

Reprinted from *Children's Songs From Japan*, Copyright Edward B. Marks Music Corporation. Used by permission.

Las Mañanitas

Es_tas son las ma_ña_ni_tas que can_ta_ba el Rey Da_

_vid pe_ro no e_ran tan bo_ni_tas co_mo las can_tan a_

_quí si el se_re_no de la es_qui_na me qui_sie_ra ha_cer fa_

_vor de a_pa_gar su lin_ter_ni_ta mien_tras que pa_sa mi a_

SOLO...

_mor.(Des_pier_ta, mi bien, des_pier_ta, mi_ra que ya a_ma_ne_

UNISON

_ció,)que a_ma_ne_ce, que a_ma_ne_ce, ro_si_ta blanca de Je_ri_

SOLO...

_có,) (des_pier_ta, mi bien, des_pier_ta, mi_ra que ya a_ma_ne_

CORO

_ció,)(ya los pa_ja_ri_llos can_tan la lu_na ya se me_

_tió, ¡que bo_ni_ta ma_ña_ni_ta! co_mo que quie_re llo_

_ver, a_sies_ta_ba la ma_ña_na, cuando te empecé a que_rer!)

118

LAS MAÑANITAS

These are like the mornings that inspired King David's songs, but never were his as beautiful as the ones we sing of here. Now if only the night watchman would extinguish the light of his lantern to make way for my love.

Chorus: Awaken my love, awaken,
       and look at the rising dawn.

It really is the break of day my little white rose of Jericho.

Chorus: Awaken my love, awaken,
       and look at the rising dawn.

The birds have broken into song while the moon turned to go inside. What a lovely morning! Though it seems it wants to rain. Towards siesta went the morning when the hour of my love for you first began.

From Venezuela

This is Your Day

(Hoy es Tu Día)

Hoy es tu día de gracia y luz; que lo ce-lebres con grande honor; que lo ce-

le-bres con a-le-grí-a que se des-bor-de del co-ra-zón. zón. Que la

di-cha te son-rí-a, entre mú-si-cas y flo-res, go-lo-si-nas y li-

co-res y espe-ran-zas en tu dí-a. Que la di-a.

HOY ES TU DÍA

"Today is your day filled with grace
       and with light:
May you celebrate it in honor
May you celebrate it in joy
That your heart be made full and run over.

May fortune smile at you
Amidst flowers and music and sweetmeats,
Nectar and hope,
Today, your own day.

May the bees make you offerings of their honey,
And dawn, the gift of its splendour.
Of nightingales receive their song,
And of cherubs their love.

May the moon encircle you with
Pearly fire,
And the stars admire you
From their rainbowed clouds."

Courtesy of the Oficina de Distribucion de Publicaciónes, Ministerio de Relaciones Exteriores, Caracas.

NAMING CHILDREN AROUND THE WORLD

The spellings given here are only approximations of the original language sounds.

AFRICA

In most of West Africa, the baby is given several names and his mother decides which he will be called by. One of his names usually designates the day of the week on which he was born. In Ghana these names are as follows:

	Boys	Girls
Sunday	Kwashie	Awushie
Monday	Kedjo	Adojoa
Tuesday	Kobla	Abla
Wednesday	Kwaku	Aku
Thursday	Kwao	Awo
Friday	Kofi	Afua
Saturday	Kwame	Ama

Popular names in Nigeria are:

	Boys	Girls
Yoruba	Bola	Ayo
Hausa	Ado	Binta
Ibo	Nwoye	Ebele
In Liberia:	Momolu	Kolu

In East Africa, the baby can be named for the time he was born or the way he was born.

In Kenya:

	Boys	Girls
Kikuyu tribe	Kamau	Rehama
Luo tribe	Okoth (he who was born when it rained)	Akelo (She who was born in the afternoon)
Masai tribe	Supati (he who was meant to be good)	Chemisi
Acholi tribe	Odoc (boy born legs first)	Adoc (girl born legs first)
In the Congo:		
Luba	Masongo	Marua

In Botwsana: Moleme (plowman) Tsholofelo (Hope)

In Ethiopia, Amharic is the official language. Some popular names are:
Kebede   Almoz
Abebe

MIDDLE EAST

In the Arab countries of the Middle East and the Moslem countries of North Africa, a common religious, linguistic and historical culture is shared, despite local variations. Therefore, the same names are popular in all the Moslem countries.

Boys	Girls	Meaning
Jamil	Jamileh	Pretty
Amal	Amal	Hope
Zaki	Zakieh	Intelligent
Sa'id	Saideh	Lucky
Habib	Habibi	Dear
Mansour	Mansourah	Victorious
Fu'ad	——	Heart
Salim	Salimeh	Safe
Farah	Farha	Joy
Achmed	Fatima	
Musa		
Ibrahim		
Ali		

In Israel, the language is Hebrew and names are drawn from Jewish tradition as well as modern Hebrew.

Biblical names:

Boys	Girls
Moshe (Moses)	D'vorah (Deborah)
David	Ruth
Joseph	Miriam
Benjamin	Sarah
Shlomo (Solomon)	Rachel
Jonathan	Rivka (Rebecca)

122

Modern Hebrew:

Chaim (life)	Elana (tree)
Shalom (peace)	Yafa (beautiful)
Aryeh, Ari (lion)	Adinah (delicate)
Judah	Rina (joy)
Israel	Shira (song)
Etan (strong)	Aviva (spring)
Asher (happy)	Aliza (happy)
	Shoshana (lily)

ASIA and the PACIFIC ISLANDS

The countries of Asia and the Pacific Islands draw their names from such a wide range of cultural, religious and historical traditions that it is impossible to choose names that are found widely in every country. Here we list names that are popular in the children's literature of some individual cultures.

	Boys	Girls
Australian		
Aborigine	Winmati	Maniya
Burma	Aung Tin	Mya Mya
Cambodia	Sothila	Vanna
Ceylon	Nihal	Anula
China	Cheng	Didi
	Wu	Liu
India	Ramu	Shakuntala
	Dhan	Lakhmi
	(rice plant)	
	Rangid	Shobhana
Indonesia	Hanji	Siti
Iran	Reza	Pari
Japan	Kazuo	Kazuko
	(Child of Peace)	
	Hideo (Ex-	Haruko
	cellent Boy)	(Child of
		Spring)
	Takeo (Boy	Megumi
	of the	(Blessing)
	Bamboo)	
Korea	Bok	Su
Laos	Somsak	Bopha
Malaysia	Mydin	Minah
Mongolia	Bator	Saran
Nepal	Kami	Tara
New Guinea	Kimo	Tarova

New Zealand-	Takona	Kuma
Maoria		
Pakistan	Mabu	Raju
Papua	Sako	Sipeta
Phillipines	Rogelio	Feliza
Thailand	Prapan	Amara
Tibet	Nema	Momo
Vietnam	Long	Mai
	(Dragon)	(Apricot)

EUROPE

In Europe the most popular names are those of the Christian saints who, the parents hope, will inspire and protect their children. The child often celebrates the saint's name day rather than his own birthday.

Here is the English name John in many languages of Europe:

Czech)	Italian—Giovanni
Dutch)	Norwegian—Johan
Flemish) Jan	Portuguese—João
Polish)	Romanian—Ion
Finnish—Juhani,	Russian—Ivan
Jaakko	Scottish—Ian, Iain
French—Jean	Serbo-Croatian—
German—Johann,	Jovan, Jovo
Hans	Swedish—John,
Greek—Yannis	Jon
Hungarian—Janos	Welsh—Evan,
Irish—Sean, Shaun,	Sion
Shane	

Here are some other popular European names:

	Boys	Girls
Austria	Maxi	Hilde
	Franz	Elisabeth,
		Liesl, Lisi
Belgium	Médard	Yvonne
	Pieter	Godelieve,
		Lieve
Bulgaria	Dmitri	Neda
Czechoslovakia	Karel	Alena
	Václav	Eva
Denmark	Palle	Inger
	Erik	Karin

England	Thomas	Anne
	Henry	Elizabeth
Finland	Niilo	Aili
	Eero	Kirsti
France	Denis	Nicole
	Jacques	Francoise
Germany	Kurt	Ursula
	Dietrich,	Erica
	Dieter	
Greece	Markos	Eleni
	Nicolaos	Penelope
Hungary	Lászlo,	Aranka
	Latsi	
	Zoltan	Zara
Iceland	Pál	Malla
	Gwender	Gunna
Ireland	Padraic,	Bridget
	Patrick	
	Brendan	Margaret,
		Peggy,
		Pegeen
Italy	Angelo	Paola
	Bruno	Gina
Netherlands	Henk	Miep
	Jaap	Annie
Norway	Reidar	Gudrun
Poland	Jerzy	Janina
	Stanislaw	Krystyna
Portugal	Henrique	Marianinha
Romania	Corneliu,	Ileana
	Nelo	
Scotland	Angus	Fiona
Sweden	Lars	Kerstin
	Bo	Gunilla
Switzerland	Gustav,	Gisela
	Gusti	
	Wilhelm,	Bettina
	Willi	
Turkey	Tarik	Ayse
Yugoslavia	Drago	Lyuba
	Branko	Mlada
U.S.S.R.	Sergei	Nina
	Alexander,	Tanya
	Sasha	
	Andrei	Lena

LATIN AMERICA

As in Europe, names are chosen from the Christian calendar of saints. Many girls have María as one of their names, and boys often have both María and Jesus. Usually children are also given other names as well, taken from literature, history or just from someone's imagination. In any case, no matter what name the child is known by, it is used in many diminutives by his older relatives and friends. This means, for example, that Miguel (Michael) can be called Miguelito (little Michael), Juana (Joan) can be called Juanita (little Joan), and so on.

Among the Indian tribes, Christian names are frequently given to children, but names in the local Indian language are also still widely used.

Some of the most widely used Spanish names are:

Boys	Girls
Luis	Luisa
Manuel	Rosa
Miguel	Josefina
Pablo	Angelita
Pedro	Carmen
Tomàs	Teresa
Felipe	Carlota

Popular names in Brazil include:

Antonio	Lilia
Paulo	Marilia

NICKNAMES AND PET NAMES

The custom of calling children not by their name but by some endearing or humorous phrase is quite common all around the world. The following picture book gives some of these phrases used in countries around the world.

MY LITTLE CABBAGE by Susan Purdy. Philadelphia, J. B. Lippincott Co., East Washington Square, Philadelphia, Pa. 19105. $2.69 net.

SUGGESTIONS FOR FURTHER READING

Stories about birthdays and ceremonies in different lands

NICOLE'S BIRTHDAY by Maud Frere. Trans. by Robin Gottlieb. Illus. by Nadine Forster. 1967. unp. $2.95; lib. binding $3.19 net. Random House, 457 Madison Avenue, New York, N.Y. 10022. Orders to: 457 Hahn Road, Westminister, Md. 21157. How a little French girl celebrates her birthday.

ONE DAY IN AZTEC MEXICO by G. Kirtland. Illus. by Jerome Snyder. 1963. 40pp. $2.50; lib. binding $2.67 net. Harcourt, Brace & World, Inc., 757 Third Avenue, New York, N.Y. 10017. An intimate glimpse of Aztec family life in a humorous story of the birth of twins to the family of a judge.

ORANGE-ROBED BOY by Patricia Wallace Garlan and Maryjane Dunstan. Illus. by Paw Oo Thet. 1967. 90pp. $4.50; lib. binding $4.13 net. Viking Press, 625 Madison Avenue, New York, N.Y. 10022. Aung Khin, a twelve year old Burmese boy, celebrates his **Shinbyu** ceremony and spends several weeks in a monastery as part of his becoming a man. Beautiful illustrations.

A WISH FOR LITTLE SISTER by Jacqueline Ayer. Illus. by the author. 1960. unp. $2.95. Harcourt, Brace & World, 757 Third Avenue, New York, N.Y. 10017. A delicately illustrated picture book which tells about the birthday of a little Thai girl.

Birthdays around the world

BIRTHDAY PARTIES AROUND THE WORLD by Barbara Rinkoff. Illus. by Doug Anderson. 1967. 210pp. $3.95. Distributed by William Morrow and Co., 425 Park Avenue South, New York, N.Y. 10016. Orders to: 788 Bloomfield Avenue, Clifton, N.J. 07012. In addition to descriptions of how birthdays are celebrated in many lands, there is a useful mail order shopping guide for international foods, decorations and toys.

BIRTHDAYS by Lillie Patterson. Illus. by Erica Merkling. 1965. 64pp. $2.32. Garrard Publishing Co., 1607 N. Market Street, Champaign, Ill. 61820. The history of birthdays and a brief glimpse of how they are celebrated today.

BOOK OF BOYS NAMES
BOOK OF GIRLS NAMES by Linwood Sleigh and Charles
Johnson. 1963. 319pp. $4.50. Thomas Y. Crowell, 201 Park
Avenue South, New York, N.Y. 10003. Each book is an
alphabetical list of favorite British names with a discus-
sion of their origins, meanings and histories. A calendar
of saints lists saints' feast days chronologically. The index
lists variant forms of each name.

HAPPY BIRTHDAYS ROUND THE WORLD by Lois S. Johnson. Illus. by Genia. 1963. 128pp. $2.95. Rand McNally,
P.O. Box 7600, Chicago, Illinois 60680. How birthdays,
name days and saints' days are celebrated in such countries as Ceylon, Iran, Nigeria and Venezuela.

PIÑATAS by Virginia Brock. Illus. by Anne Marie Jauss. 1966.
106pp. $3.00. Abingdon Press, 201 Eighth Avenue South,
Nashville, Tenn. 37202. This book tells how piñatas began
and how to make them. There are also three amusing
stories featuring pinatas.

Cradle songs and birthday poems

BIRTHDAY CANDLES BURNING BRIGHT; A TREASURY
OF POETRY selected by Sara and John E. Brewton. 1960.
199pp. $3.95. MacMillan Co., 866 Third Avenue, New York,
N.Y. 10022. American and British poems about birth, names,
birthdays, twins and growing.

LULLABIES OF THE WORLD by Dorothy Berliner Commins.
1967. 266pp. $12.95. Random House, 457 Madison Avenue,
New York, N.Y. 10022. Orders to: 457 Hahn Road, West-
minster, Md. 21157. Almost 150 lullabies from many cultures, presented in native script, transliteration and English
translation. Explanatory notes and piano settings.

About the world's religions and their prophets

ALLAH, THE GOD OF ISLAM; MOSLEM LIFE AND WOR-
SHIP by Florence Mary Fitch. Illus. with photos. 1950. 144pp.
$3.95; lib. binding $3.70 net. Lothrop, Lee & Shepard Co.,
Inc., 381 Park Avenue South, New York, N.Y. 10017. Orders
to: Wilmor Warehouse, 788 Bloomfield Avenue, Clifton,
N.J. 07012

BUDDHA by Joan Lebold Cohen. Illus. by Mary Frank. 1969.
96pp. $3.95; lib. binding $3.69 net. Delacorte Press, 750
Third Avenue, New York, N.Y. 10017. The life of the
founder of Buddhism, told in a style that captures the
flavor of the East.

MOHAMMED: PROPHET OF THE RELIGION OF ISLAM
by E. Royston Pike. 1969. $3.95. Frederick A. Praeger, 111

Fourth Avenue, New York, N.Y. 10003. The story of Mohammed's life with an introduction to the teachings of the Koran and the faith of Islam.

HOW THE GREAT RELIGIONS BEGAN by Joseph Gaer. 1956. 424pp. $5.00. Dodd, Mead & Co., 79 Madison Avenue, New York, N.Y. 10016. Paper (Signet P2253), $.60. New American Library, 1301 Avenue of the Americas, New York, N.Y. 10019. The life stories of Jesus, Moses, Lao-tse, Zoroaster, Mahavira, Mohammed, Buddha, Confucius and Kabir are accompanied by statements about the religion founded by each.

THE PRINCE WHO GAVE UP A THRONE; A STORY OF THE BUDDHA by Nancy Serage. Illus. by Kazue Mizumura. 1966. 62pp. $3.50. Thomas Y. Crowell, 201 Park Avenue South, New York, N.Y. 10003. How Buddha renounced a rich kingdom to seek illumination.

RELIGIONS AROUND THE WORLD by Leonard and Carolyn Wolcott. Illus. by Gordon Laite. 1967. 191pp. $4.95. Abingdon Press, 201 Eighth Avenue South, Nashville, Tenn. 37202. An examination of the world's great religions, and a discussion of the emerging religions today.

TALES AND LEGENDS FROM INDIA by Iris MacFarlane. Illus. by Eric Thomas. 1965. 136pp. $3.95. Franklin Watts, 575 Lexington Avenue, New York, N.Y. 10022. A delightful selection of ten tales dealing with kings, gods and young men. Chapter seven tells of the birth of Lord Krishna.

THEIR SEARCH FOR GOD; WAYS OF WORSHIP IN THE ORIENT by Florence Mary Fitch. Illus. with photos. 1947. $3.50; lib. binding $3.35 net. 160pp. Lothrop, Lee & Shepard Co., Inc., 381 Park Avenue South, New York, N.Y. 10017. Orders to: Wilmor Warehouse, 788 Bloomfield Avenue, Clifton, N.J. 07012. Photographs and descriptions of the Hindu, Confucian, Taoist, Shinto and Buddhist religions.

THE TREE OF LIFE; SELECTIONS FROM THE LITERATURE OF THE WORLD'S RELIGIONS, edited by Ruth Smith. 1942. 496pp. $6.00; lib. binding $5.63 net. Viking Press, 625 Madison Avenue, New York, N.Y. 10022. Moving and important passages from the scriptures and prayers of the world's great religions.

THE WORLD'S GREAT RELIGIONS by the Editors of **Life**. Illus. with photos and drawings. 1957. $4.95; paper $2.45. Golden Press, 850 Third Avenue, New York, N.Y. 10022. Orders to: 1220 Mound Avenue, Racine, Wisconsin 53404. Two hundred color photographs illustrate the succinct descriptions of Christianity, Judaism, Islam, Buddhism, Hinduism and the Chinese philosophies.

INDEX

128